YES NO MAYBE

by Glen Brown

cover design: Chris Grodoski
layout editor: Wayne Spelius
editor: Carol Spelius
staff assistant, Anne Brashler

LAKE SHORE PUBLISHING

373 Ramsay Road,

Deerfield, IL 60015

ISBN # 0-941363-37-6
Copyright 1995
price $9.95

Introduction by Lucia Cordell Getsi

From transposing fairy tale heroines out of their mythic cloth cut to psychic truth into the stutter of repetitive contemporary urban scenes, and from transposing the humdrums of contemporary urban life into something approaching a tongue-in-cheek mythic significance, Glen Brown sets us down hard beyond the antipodes of *yes* and *no* into the land of *maybe*, where hope and doubt routinely change places. *Maybe* is what comes from a 1950's childhood on Chicago's Elizabeth Street and parenting and teaching in the 1990's suburbs. *Maybe* is where we are all living, which is why the poems in this book will bring readers painful shivers of recognition as well as pleasure.

Lucia Cordell Getsi

Illinois Author of the Year, 1994
Author of INTENSIVE CARE
Editor of *The Spoon River Poetry Review*

Acknowledgments

Grateful acknowledgments are made to the editors of the following publications in which some of these poems, sometimes in different versions, first appeared:

American Goat, Ariel, California Quarterly, The Cape Rock, Damaged Wine, Fan, Great River Review, Hammers, The Illinois Review, Mediphors, Negative Capability, Oyez Review, Pearl, Poet & Critic, Prairie Light Review, Right Brain Review, Slipstream, South Coast Poetry Journal, The Spoon River Poetry Review, Tamaqua, Willow Review, Windless Orchard, TROIKA V (Thorntree Press), and *Poetry* ("Maybe", copyright 1992, The Modern Poetry Assoc.)

Foreword by James Langlas

When we read the poetry we enjoy, most of us hope to get a glimpse of the poet as human being -- an up-close, personal glimpse. Glen Brown's YES NO MAYBE gives us what we want. Indeed, in these poems, we see Glen Brown the man, and we learn to embrace his insight.

The poems in this collection let us consider the twists and turns of life. For starters, he allows us to see some fairy tale characters as modern victims, and the inconsistencies of life begin to haunt us as we view the bloodshed in "Sanctuary" and the poverty in "Double Vision." However, what makes Glen Brown's poems so striking is his ability to take us back into pleasure and reverie, as well as into the moments when we give "pitch-perfect responses each day" or "drift perpetually in memory."

The fact that so many of us can take our own experiences into these poems pulls them all together and makes us love them. Glen Brown ultimately places us in the family where we, either as children or as parents, discover something about ourselves and the way the world works. His wonderful poem "Maybe" prepares us for all of the possibilities and points to the dynamics of families -- the pain and expectation, the love and the hope. When we travel through the difficulties of childhood and into the joys of parenthood, we see that YES NO MAYBE reminds us "what the heart has known forever" and gives us the feeling that we can all come out on top.

James Langlas is the English chairman at Wheaton North High School as well as a poet and a 5th degree Black Belt in Tae Kwon-Do.

He has been published in *Poetry, American Scholar*, and *Cutbank*. He is also recipient of two grants from the Illinois Arts Council.

Dedication

For my children and their children . . .
and for my wife

Table of Contents

I -- Yes, No, Maybe

II -- Tending the Hearth

I

Yes, No, Maybe

RIDING RAPUNZEL

One day a beautiful woman bolted out
of bewildering love, entered
the wider circumference of her loneliness
and let down her golden hair
for men to climb on trysts.

She galloped into their lives
like the trumpet's shocking blare
at the starting gate,
built a small fire in each of their hearts
and slept far from her wedding vows,
while the outlines of morning smoothed
to gray afternoons.

She let her hair fall over
her dove-white breasts,
sipped straight from each breath
the rampion taste of truth,
found it unfamiliar as her race with lies,
until one day she broke her stride,
cantered upon the thin ice
of an early thaw of marriage
and drowned herself in a blue tower --
the mistress of sad, fairy-tale luck.

RED RIDING HOOD BUYS TERM LIFE

The plot is flawed, the dialogue unbelieveable;
the characters lack a compulsive trait.
Why not make him an insurance salesman
in a blazing blue oxford and paisley tie,
pump him up with instant coffee and breath mints
and line the inside of his gray sportcoat
with appointments and ball-point pens?
As for Red wearing the velvet coat
her ex-lover gave her, black tights and heels,
add a pouting mouth, legs of a flight attendant
and the endurance of a triathlon athlete.

Now put them downtown with the Budweiser horses
panting around a clock in a smoke-filled bar,
Johnny Mathis songs and three dollar beer calls.
And let's say she doesn't have a florist's heart
for long-stemmed roses or daffodils,
drink imported wines or eat French pastries.
Rather the evening is the scent of loud perfume,
dizzy with come-ons and pitchers of beer,
their conversation stale as the popcorn and Frito-lay.
We know the odds, a thousand to one,
like the first day of baseball tryouts.
But he's determined, and she's willing
with firm adolescent glands --

lust floating in his brain and love in hers.

Oh, I'll spare you the happiness forever after,
a-little-lost-girl-saved-by-a-prince routine.
They wake up with separation swirling in their hearts,
lost in a forest of ordinary in the haze of day,
lying with the promise to see each other again.
But he knows, rises out of bed,
fumbles with his watch band, counts the bills
in his billfold to make sure, then straightens his tie
while she brushes her hair, her bare arm
twitching like a machine as the door clicks shut.

SNOW WHITE TURNS 40

Oh, Snow White, eternal housewife,
you should have danced all night
in your step-mother's red-hot iron shoes.
She knew that a woman's face mattered enough
to tell lies, worked her own with Oil of Olay.
Did you think the men in your life
wouldn't want a beautiful housewife too?

You could have married that huntsman,
slept on the forest floor
or lived with the wild boar and saved your heart
from the bottomless hours of housework and whoring
for those seven little men, the moments in between
when you watched your sigh-long tale of woe
thicken like porridge.

Had you not puked out the last of your luck
when your prince arrived,
the tea kettle wouldn't be steaming with anger,
misting old desires into clotheslines out back
while your hands conspire
against the polygraphic lines around your eyes
reflected in the looking-glass upon your wall.

CINDERELLA DANCING

In America, it's black high-tops,
and cobbler's wax won't hold them down.
She drives a red Pontiac Grand Am in a vinyl mini,
works shifts at Corrugated Box Incorporated
for twice minimum wage.
On weekends, she boogies her prince 'til dawn,
her brow boiling like water,
her feet tireless on the dance hall parquet.
She burns her lust to cinders,
sleeps among the ashes to noon
in a brass-framed bed.

This is a new-world doll locked in uppercase,
a Madonna in Technicolor
rolling boyfriends like stones.
There are no hazel twigs for her devotion,
no pigeon houses or pear trees to hide in,
just Houdini wrapped in the straightjacket of self
sealed in a cardboard ego,
born into a world already made to order.

BRIAR ROSE DEFUNCT

There's not much you can say to a woman
who thinks she's slept for 100 years,
launched from a century of dreams
with just a kiss.
And it doesn't matter; her breath is bad.

Outside, condos have erupted from the ground,
and the evening sky is pocked with fewer stars.
I hand her a long-stemmed rose;
it's thornless. And I ask her to marry me,
knowing all the while that no insurance company
will cover another coma like this.

With "Who the hell are you?" bursting
from her lips, brittle with the senselessness of ice,
I know the anesthetic has worn off,
but her amnesia hasn't. It makes me think
about the physics in all this, the coming light
about to pour through a hole in her universe,
how evolution will never be the same.

And I cannot remember
how the story is supposed to end:
why the flies were asleep
on the walls and the horses in their stables,
the brindled hounds in the yard, even the doves,
their heads tucked under their wings.

But that was another story,
and it doesn't take long to discover
that nothing consoles quite like an eternity
of dreamless nights.

Now she's mumbling something about insomnia,
and I slip out, my knees spilling
into a gurney wheeling down the hall
with the sheet pulled over,
my hands grasping the answer in an instant.

BARTLEBY THE SCRIVENER

Ah Bartleby! Ah humanity!

... Herman Melville

Perhaps he lost the language of desire,
hope checking out first
with its twin baggage *want* and *need,*
hunger leaving no forwarding address.

Or maybe the language of protocol
surrendered its meaning,
the tongue holding *diplomacy* hostage
behind a green folding screen.

Presume he was stunned into silence
by God's loneliness, by the fixed stare
of the black wall just beyond
the small side-window courting a dim light.

So much to *prefer not to* while the grass
and sky stitched together a singular void,
and the bud of Existentialism took root,
denial sprouting from him

like some metaphysical joke told in reverse.
He knew nothingness soon becomes
a stranger to no one; preferring it
was like telling the punchline first.

JUST IN TIME
OR ANOTHER URBAN TALL-TALE

The plant was breathing heavily.
She had just brought it home
from the garden center,
a barrel-shaped cactus with a waxy skin,
its two-foot spine clustered with barbed wire.

She put it on the shelf next to the organ pipe,
saguano and Mexican pincushion
and thought nothing about the shuddering at first,
its wide, fleshy stem expanding
and contracting like an accordian.

She knew about cacti, how they swell
to hold water, but the soil was too dry.
The emergency call rang through
the garden center:
"My cactus seems alive," she said.

"Get out of the house," they warned her.
And within minutes, three men arrived
with thick, vinyl bags.
They encased the plant,
just before it burst open like a detonated cocoon,

seconds before the bags were catapulted
by a thousand, microscopic hairs
from a hundred, unburrowed tarantulas
injecting, macerating and sucking the plastic
that bound the one-chambered ovary.

DON'T ASK WHY

"We're going in through here," he says
with a Neil Armstrong drawl
pointing to a wall chart
of the lower digestive tract.
". . . up the sigmoid and descending colon,
through the transverse,
then down the ascending colon."
Nothing contradictory about that, I think,
just four small steps . . .

Yes, at moments like this,
lunar dust lies against the slopes of rocks
never before trekked, nebulas remain
unfathomed and quasars unseen.
Here, though, sandblasted by a gallon of Colyte,
that instant salt and polyethylene punch,
he will see across distant, soft linings
with a myopic pipe of flexible fibers
that beams light, elbows images
back to an eyepiece, milli-seconds away.

"We'll take some biopsies," he adds.
". . . probably just pseudo-polyps anyway."
And I'm turned on my left side
in a shift made for these occasions.

Two tubes bullwhip from my nose;
the I.V. probing my right arm
erases both sensation and memory.

This is something like self-mockery:
life is a hoax, a gift marked by chance
explorations and clichés. Look,
there are black holes sucking light out there,
galaxies exploding at warp speed.
"May the force be with you,"
I murmur before the light goes out.

THE CHECKUP
(Symphony for the Dental Hygienist)

It's the waiting that intimidates you,
the walls shelved with pamphlets --
root canal treatment, gum disease,
X-ray safety. Then the office door
opens with an overture of nerves,
and she alarms you by name.
Your feet, Novocaine numb
from crossing, press down the Indian bed of nails.
What you didn't forget is the chair,
doctor's office vinyl
with a head and body tilt for excavating.
Of course there are the instruments,
plastic-wrapped on the metal tray
along side the latex gloves and gauzy mask.

But it begins with X-rays, an *allegro*
for two cardboard wings
and the slight gag reflex;
then your memory is jarred loose
with sounds of the scaler,

an *andante* of scraping
and foraging for bacon bits
and orange pulp. Your mouth
is fixed in a capital *O;* the saliva ejector
hangs under your tongue
trapped in the maelstrom.
The lamp beams down just beneath
the ceiling mobile of paper boats.
There's nowhere else to stare except at this

and her face.
By now you know the subtle shades of her eyes
better than you know your wife's,
the number of blemishes on her forehead
and other indelicacies.

She lavages with the cavitron, *con moto moderato*,
eradicating cola and tea stains
with a crescendo to rival timpani,

then the finale of flossing and electric brushing,
an *allegretto* of rinsing and sucking,
the metallic taste flowing from molars and bicuspids
raked and plowed clean.

It all comes down to the *maestro*,
the virtuoso's work and then the checkup.
"I'll see you in six months" sounds like applause,
and you whisk out the door *vivace!*
with a new tooth brush and floss in hand
and with no encore.

PETER STUBBS PACKS UP AND FLEES TO CHICAGO VIA TIME MACHINE TO ESCAPE BAD PRESS

Pursued by the mob of townspeople
and the shaky glow of their torches,
he finds refuge crouching under a mossy bridge
                                    --Billy Collins

Imagine somewhere in Chicago
he takes out the folded *Tribune* ad
stuffed loosely in his shrunken trousers
with growling, snarling defiance,
his restless, furtive eyes glowing
under the hazy light of the full moon.
"Call a Gregory Clinic today for permanent removal
of unwanted facial and body hair..." It reads.

What could this be, he wonders.
He had petitioned the devil,
even omitted the parsley from his cauldron
of hemlock, opium and henbane,
hoping for smoother, hair-free skin.
And now he was only a phone call away!

Imagine his brilliant, white teeth flashing
beneath his yellow-green eyes,
dark patches of fur standing on end
as he reads about the International Academy

of Professional Electrologists, modern alchemists
with state-of-the-art technology.

More effective than rye, mistletoe and yew,
he supposes. It's time to escape
certain beheading, the ubiquity of legend
and the bad PR that folklore had produced
these past four hundred years.

"Sure I'm a bit overzealous at times
with some girls, but linking lycanthropy
and parthenophagy is iconoclastic,"
he mutters to himself.

Near a telephone booth, somewhere in Chicago,
he paces wildly in circles.
He removes his wolf-skin belt,
rolls around in the dirt three times, then dusts off
his soiled trousers. A cloud crosses the moon
as he begins to dial...

SUBURBAN LOCKUP

The door handle is just below eye-level.
A dead-bolt is where the handle should be.
The storm door slams airtight,
a black, Mediterranean iron with no screen.
Everything is keyed from inside:
the doors, windows and metal grates
across the basement windows.
They used to seat a mannequin
on the couch downstairs,
an expressionless dummy
fashioned in a wig and kimono,
the *National Enquirer* placed on its lap.
The neighborhood voyeur
might have been seduced
had he peeked through the windows;
the night burglar
might have tripped alarms in his head
about the tenants --
maybe they're kinky or lunatics
with a hidden gun wired to spring
from a moving hinge.

The German Shepherd growls
metallically from her cage.
She grinds bones down with animal ease.
Legs would be no contest for her,
just pretzel sticks in a hot vicegrip.
Yet the house is dark, inviting
the random thief off the streets.

The living room, like a Slingerland drum set,
sparkles silver glitter; the dining room
reflects dimly in smoke mirrors
a parlor of '50s furniture,
flock paper and dark paneling.

A statue of Rebecca at the Well
stands by the front door propped shut
by a cane buttressing the door handle
just beneath the two dead-bolts and chainlock.
The house is a labyrinth of alarms,
an ambush of latches,
constructed from fears of the Great Depression,
WW II and the nightly news -- a million hands
warming over garbage drums,
hungry eyes in ski masks.

SANCTUARY

New York-- A naked man, carrying red carnations,
ran into St. Patrick's Cathedral . . .
He killed one man and injured a police officer
before being shot to death . . .

--from a news story

We might have imagined him straight-edging
his wrists, plunging from bridge
to water, the .22 ricocheting
off the back of his skull,

or his feet dangling above the floor.
Instead he chose absolution
in another form of suicide.
He took off his clothes at 50th Street

and Rockefeller Plaza.
He entered the Manhattan shrine
where the air charged with incense;
the votive candles flickered orange,

and the inscrutable, soft murmurings
of prayer rose from the front pews.
The parishioners gasped
at the iron prayer bookstand

crushing down upon the usher's back.
But he believed that he was Christ
purging the temple from sinners,

chanting a dark monologue,

expunging demons or exorcising his own.
And he discarded his life in the streets
because he wanted something unattainable:
refuge, testimony or God.

He was gunned down in the middle aisle
of the cathedral, his sepulcher
the fringed petals spilling blood
at the foot of the altar.

DÍA DE LOS MUERTOS

*Chalma, Mexico -- At least 41 worshippers were suffo-
cated or crushed to death when a tightly packed crowd
began pushing and shoving at a church famed for a religious icon believed to have miraculous powers. Thirteen
of the victims were children.*

-- from a news story

They came from Guadalupe and Guasave
and from villages in the south
with prayer on their tongues,
across nameless plains and mountains
in borrowed automobiles full of parcels
of hope and faith, their lives pawned
for one more pilgrimage.

Little children in their Sunday suits
and starched, white cotton dresses;
young, barefooted women
in embroidered bodices and lacy headdresses;
their mustachioed men in huaraches and doeskin;
and the old: tortilla-breasted and stern-faced
in dark shawls, fingering beads pressed together.
Like a pile of sapodilla seeds,
they gathered at the sanctuary
with garlands of marigolds and chrysanthemum,
hoping for a cure.

There was a loud perfume of bougainvillea
rising among the festoons,
the Virgin enticing them to come closer,

and then an avalanche of bodies --
the terrible stomping
and crushing of skulls and bones
two-and-a-half tons of trust
beneath the shrine, one afternoon
under the hemorrhaging, Mexican sun,
the red sky burning in their eyes.

DOUBLE VISION

*Caracas-- Venezuelan police arrested a doctor and
eleven city morgue employees on suspicion of removing
the eyes from corpses and selling them for corneal trans-
plants to a doctor in Maracay who was charging up to
$2000 . . .*

--from a news story

Now that he has new eyes
a mosaic of phosphenes
becomes his corneal slide show.
The scarlet ibis,
cuckoo and Orinoco crocodile,
some ten million different color surfaces
emerge in an Andes panorama.

But suppose he's a rich
white man in Maracay
with these dry Mestizo eyes,
these freedom-fighter eyes
with a retina of debt and anger.
Will they flash high-rise ranchos
or sharecropping black gold
from Lake Maracaibo?
Does he dine with the provincial elite,
protesting the Populist with a master plan?

And suppose while staring
into his vegetable stew, plantains,
cacao, and slabs of beef
or while dancing the guaracha

his optic nerves trigger the insides
of a squatter settlement
outside Caracas, or the faces
of children in barrios
across coastal lowlands?

Maybe he sees an ophthalmologist
for artificial tears
or a psychiatrist for photophobia.
Maybe he kneels before
some Roman Catholic priest
or the weeping Madonna
begging for the miracle
of eyes that cry.

CONTEMPLATION ON A CAT CROSSING HIGHWAY 435 AT 4 A.M. IN KANSAS CITY

He may have come upon dozens
of roadkills himself in his nine lives
without reflecting, dodged hundreds
of Kansas license plates and returned safely
to wherever his cat instinct dictated.
But what he was doing
on this channel of highway
locked in the cross hairs of headlight beams
535 miles from Chicago
at precisely that moment my car reeled forward,
juxtaposing cruise control, refueling
and road construction with energy, motion
and velocity -- a colossal calibration
for a near miss -- may have some universal
significance for philosophy or calculus.
Call it metaphysics or mathematics.
By any other name, it was luck.

NOT QUITE A SONNET ON THE DIVISIBILITY OF KINETICS AND INFINITE BISECTION OR A THEORY OF YARDWORK

I can not help musing as the ancient
philosophers, such indolent meta-
physicians with nothing to do all day:
hulking Heraclitus with both feet sub-
merged in the same river, soaking bunions
in a flux to prove his Logos; drunken
Zeno, denying motion by proving
nondivisibility in goblets
of wine. All this while there's work to be done:
the grass needs mowing, the viburnum needs
pruning. No doubts about this collision
of leaf and blade. I think I'll leave the lawn
half-cut, the bushes half-trimmed and venture
upon this dialectic in my yard.

HUM IF YOU CAN'T SING

So what if at every turn in life we burst
into song -- thoughtless as reciting a prayer --
reward our feet with a waltz or two,

congratulate ourselves with an aria
then tap dance our way through
the kitchen and dining room?

And suppose the musicians arrive
early each morning
to tune up their strings, oil their drums

while the white-gloved conductor
waits with his cue sheet at the breakfast table?
Could we expect a chorus

prophesying disaster
or an overture announcing a new business deal?
Why not ask for a drum roll through toiletry

or a diminuendo through dinner?
And what might our friends say
about all that sheet music stuffed in our pants

pockets, about our lives
cluttered with voice lessons

and rehearsals with girls in fishnet?

Imagine the fun of it all,
the spotlight on us as we dance and sing,
our pets joining in with happy tails

and the birds whistling from their cages,
encouraging applause
for our pitch-perfect responses each day.

HELL

The sinners of the last round
lie completely sealed in ice . . .
-- Canto XXXIV, Circle 9: The Inferno

You've heard the jokes
about the insurance salesman and some guy
locked in a soundproof eight-by-ten cell,
or the one about being stalled in traffic
with your mother-in-law and her choir of tongues,
the windows cranked up and with no heat.

In grammar school, the old Irish priest
told us the walls were
"four thousand miles thick,"
that the fire was without seam and everlasting
like a Latin teacher's conjugation of verbs.

But I always thought it was the way
Hieronymus Bosch saw it
with special effects, vapors and strobe lights,
or like being trapped
with an eternity of Munch's screamers,
their faces dripping that dripless wax.

Today it's a used car salesman
who won't give you back your car keys,
or the hail of "Have a nice day"
from the cashier buffing her nails,
you looking up from the circle of ice,
the defroster in your car still not working.

EUCLID AND BARBIE

Math class is tough

-- Barbie

Sure it doesn't add up:
countless camping and skiing trips with Ken,
swimming and skating parties without danger,
dancing and shopping engagements
with Midge and Skipper
like an infinite summer vacation.
Nothing here hints at a dull math class
for integral Barbie and her complex playmates!
Even her curvaceous body
proves mathematically impossible.
She's an isosceles bimbo
with the whole greater than the sum of her parts.
Just bend her at an obtuse angle,
press her into her pink Porsche
and watch her scud across miles of linoleum
or catapult down the stairs.
You'll know that her appeal
is an equation of Euclidean beauty and speed.
She doesn't need school.
She was created to multiply
fantasy by freedom in every young girl's mind.
Why be upset when Barbie says,
"Math class is tough"?
You can always add for her --
the numberless accessories
to her version of the American dream.

KEEPING A NET BENEATH THEM

To teach is one of three impossible jobs.
                                    --Freud

I open the book, pump four poems into their heads,
push a paper ladder against their brains
and beg them to climb out of their mind-set
of sex, rock 'n' roll and alcohol.
But I discover their fear of heights.
And of course, I compete with MTV,
their day dreaming, and the strawberry blonde
in a Saran Wrap costume snorkeling for attention.
Once I drowned in the undertow of mini-skirts,
bell-bottom trousers and long hair row after row.
So maybe it makes no difference now
what they think or wear in public school,
whether they *squeeze the universe into a ball*
to roll it toward some overwhelming question
or *love a red wheelbarrow glazed with rainwater*
beside the white chickens. These are city kids!
They buy their Grade A eggs in cardboard cartons,
plumb the depths of their lives without sweetness
and with weekend scores. And what they learn
surges in 30 second sound bites of beer
and designer wear. Perhaps they'll find out later
all they need to know about *truth beauty,*
now riptides to their fleeting desires.
Still I can't help but love their vertigo,
the heavy tug of ignorance lifting slowly
from their faces against the sinking of gravity,
just after they chance upon that first rung
and ascend with no sense of balance.

"THE DEVIL'S WHORE"
(for John Dickson)

Nothing could have prepared us
for that first day of class:
our libidos impaled suddenly
by a film of copulating mantids
behind a Chinese elm,

the female's slender body
with wings like leaves,
rotating head and bulging eyes.
We soon discovered the thorax of love,
how her posturing of praying

and quivering foreplay
turned to a quick thrust of spiny forelegs,
locking him in a cloak of bug lust.
We could not help but wonder
what drew him to her

for his one flight of ecstasy,
that he would continue to mate
long after his head was devoured
by her biting mandibles.
"The devil's whore," the teacher called her.

No one asked the question,
and we filed quietly out of the room.
The girls, whispering,
appeared to sway down the hall
while we, bug-eyed, quickly passed them.

VOLUPTUOUS WOMEN
(after Stephen Dunn)

They are not like other women,
and they know it.
They make us tremble,
hold our breath, wheel and fantasize.
Everything is put on hold
when they enter a room.
Motion defies time, and we moan.

They suffer for this special advantage,
for needing our reassurance,
and we know that it's better to treat them
as if they were unexceptional,
like the freckled-face girl next door.
They'll be surprised
by our indifference, relieved
of having to put forth an effort.
They might allow us to approach,
attend to what we might ask,
offer us their loneliness in return
for not soliciting.

And lucky we will be
to have had such women in our lives
when years from now we unplug our lust
and drift perpetually in memory.

THE PERPETUAL SINGULARITY
OF EXPERIENCE

I stood still like Heraclitus
in the flux of a shopping rush.
You wore the clothes
and expression of someone else now.
Thoughts poured from a zip-locked memory:
a romance like a search-and-destroy mission,
a relationship of mines
detonated years afterward
from a slammed door and silent unforgiving.

Life is filled with graves,
and there you were exiting the bookstore,
exhumed from a past
buried by other liaisons.
You fumbled with your purse,
a clutter of packages, gloves, keys.
I stood under the fluorescent lamps,
my hand balancing
on the spines of mysteries,
witnessed by a thousand eyes.

But my eyes were fixed upon you
like a voyeur waiting between the stacks
hoping for surprise.
And when you left, I stepped
into the flow of shoppers again,
but not in the same place twice.

JUST BEFORE OVULATION

They suck the blood
of a mammal
so their eggs will develop properly.
Without blood, the females die.

All night they hunt inside,
cruising like Harrier jets
for warm blood,
landing like dust upon my flesh
to siphon a meal
with hypodermic bites.
The room buzzes
with their spiracular singing.

They stick to the walls
like tiny, cluster bombs --
thin exoskeletons
splattered by a bath towel.

I lie next to you, waiting
for another sortie,
guarding your centerfold innocence,
leaving your sex unemployed.
It puzzles me
that they leave you alone.
How do they know?

SPILT MILK

I love the ruins in Rome,
those granite columns, domes
and arches of megalomania:
the Pantheon, Forum, Basilica
and Colosseum. I am fond
of things broken up,
toppled relationships with women,
like dominoes, one after another.
I love rained-out ball games,
swamping a pitcher's mound,
rolling tarpaulins,
the ricochet of lightning striking
flag poles, the jagged floss
of light, then the Zildjian sound.
I love cakes that don't rise,
burnt dinners, the look
in my wife's smoked-filled eyes,
"Oh, shit!" slipping from her lips.
I love old men's faces
worn like maps, their leathery hands,
the stories they tell one another
over and over, but never
the same way twice.
I live with ruinous things:
hand-me-downs, where loss
becomes gain, and memories
tangle like hair brushed from combs.

THE IN-LAWS

They hold the coffee pot hostage
for five mornings
and kidnap spoons without ransom.
They bring their own gin and tonic
for evenings, and they stack up
more dirty dishes than a hospital cafeteria.
It's summer visitation again,
and they're here from Junction City, Kansas,
complete with accents, gifts from Walmart
and embarrassing cucumbers, tomatoes
the size of grapefruits.
Each morning my wife prepares
three pots of Extra Premium;
then she walks to the grocery store
for donuts, fruit pie and the daily newspaper.
He spies the Market Report;
his wife recites Dear Abbey.
By afternoon the TV's booming,
and the early evening dinner
with six-packs of imported beer,
stirs the barbecue out of hibernation.
Conversation blows tornadoes and heat;
everything else is "thing-a-ma-jigs"
and "what-cha-ma-call-its."
When they leave, it's the ceremonial
hugs and kisses from my wife and children;
I do the same, thinking all the while
about next year, vowing paper plates,
styrofoam cups, plastic spoons, Lite Beer,
and a large bottle of Nescafe.

YES

It's the high-five of words
with a swish of sound,
an affirmation of what is
and what might come.
In one small breath,
it can change us with its pledge.
Its covenant, sometimes superstitious,
like crossing one's heart
or kissing the book,
locks us to the future.

Yes is the adverbial wishbone of fate,
an affidavit of hope,
washing, like a tidal wave,
politics into history,
geography into space.

NO

We say it when all else fails,
and we are at nerve's end.
It's a proud word with an emphatic *O*,
said with light speed.
The exclamation bursts
like a dark fist from our tongues.

No is an unambiguous disclaimer,
shouting miles away from *maybe,*
light years from *yes.*
It's a stubborn word
bellowing from the larynx and oral cavity.
Yet, *no* needs repeating
like learning a foreign language
or the multiplication table for the first time.

It's a saucy adverb,
the least breath of sound
smarting like Jalapeños against the palate,
and it leaves no doubt.

MAYBE

It's a word full of promise, a word like sex
ringing with possibility
like a second, sidelong glance,
a cousin of *perhaps,* a distant relative of *chance*
with no present, without guarantee,
a nondescript meaning with a built-in mortality
but more alluring than *yes*
and not as confident as *no.*

Maybe puts us on parole, sentencing us
with ellipses, hurling us into doubt
where imagination becomes as thrilling
as the goal itself. It's a word ready to lie,
an adverbial paradox full of hope.
It keeps us hungry, and we say it
to our children and loved ones
because it's less harsh than *no*
but not quite *yes,* knowing all along
it will be one or the other.

II

Tending the Hearth

A SIMPLER TIME

The four of us lived in a two-room flat
for fifteen dollars a month
where the floors sagged
from the weight of a wine press
and wine barrels that were once kept there.

Water rushed diagonally then dammed up
against the room's west wall
when mom scrubbed the linoleum floor.
(Not even Lysol could remove
the perfume of fermented grapes.)

After work each day, dad went to a bath house
on Grand Avenue; we bathed
in a twenty-five gallon tub
heated with continuous pots of cold water
on the oil stove.

We kept our food in a fruit crate from A & P.
He hammered it outside the window,
just out of reach of the alley cats
and sewer rats.
We lived on Race Street for fourteen months

where I slept in a crib
opposite a glass-dividing door,
and where just beyond
another family lived out its life in 1951
with clear voices in silhouettes parallel to ours.

The smell of grapes filled the rooms,
and we were drunk with happiness.

THE DAY AFTER VITO'S
(for my sister "Pidge")

He was a left-handed Tarzan
swinging from Addante's grocery store awning.
His right hand waved a .22 caliber pistol,
and shots rang out on Race and Elizabeth Street,
Father's Day, 1957.
The Everly Brothers were singing
"Bye, Bye Love" on the Philco;
Rocky Marciano abandoned his title
the year before,
and this was just another Sunday brawl
between mom and dad.

The day after Vito's Tavern brought no surprises
for my sister and me, but this time
mom broke my plastic guitar over his head
heavy with 80 proof,
and we had to duck through alleys
and down gangways
to avoid his Fairlane's squealing tires.

Why was he chasing us?
How was I to know about the effects
of Early Times and Blatz beer at six-years-old?
He tried to leave mom before,
and he made my sister lug suitcases
down the front stairs while I listened to cursing
and the neighbors listening,
their doors slightly ajar.

We cried because of his almost leavetaking.
He said, ". . . not even a box of White Owl cigars . . ."
and ". . . let's go to the Sox game."

But he passed out just in time,
and my sister dragged his suitcases
up the stairs until next time.

Mom didn't speak to him for four days,
and he made me his mediator with a mission
to obtain her mercy.
By Saturday, the two of them were going to Vito's,
and "I'm All Shook Up" was playing
on Dick Clark's American Bandstand.

A CHILDHOOD RECIPE
(for Dorothy Eonni)

It hit us like a freight train
the moment we opened the downstairs
door leading to the hallway --
a slow, continuous potpourri
of oregano, Parmesan
and garlic cloves fried in olive oil.
The entire building simmered in it.

Like an Italian sculptress,
mom kneaded ground beef,
grated cheese, crackers and eggs
into meatballs the size of small plums.
All day long, she labored over dough
and ricotta with a pinch of parsley and basil.
She rolled it into ravioli,
small squares carved by a wheelcutter.
Her fingers left ribbons
of flour on the table.

We kept Sundays with an eight-quart pot
of Contadina paste, hot sausages,
tomatoes, beef neckbones
and pizza bread from Atlas Bakery
hand-dipped in her red gravy,
the long wooden spoon mixing
steam into the air.

FIVE YEARS BEFORE PETE ROSE

I bought a box of baseball cards
at Tessie's candy store
on Elizabeth Street for two dollars,
forty packs frosted in glucose
and a yield of players
we'd swap like big-league
managers making trades.

Sometimes two or three Ernie Banks'
cards turned up in one box,
a bait for any Cubs addict in '58.
I was the only White Sox fan
on Elizabeth Street that year,
a pariah who went to Wrigley Field
carrying a bag of peanut butter

sandwiches for munching,
baseball cards for autographs
and gum for wagering with enemies
on the game's outcome.
We'd always arrive just in time
for batting practice; I'd cheer
for the challenger in town --

Reds, Dodgers, Phillies,
it didn't matter -- amid jeers.
I'd bet forty sticks of gum
against the Cubs each game,
come home overdosed on sugar,
my jaws sore from chewing.

THE NEED TO TELL SOMEONE

I wish I could live
someone else's poem, maybe
fight over a ham sandwich
with a bony street cat in Rome
along side Gerald Stern of New Jersey,
or live in New York and watch
Dorothy Blake spit another long line
of phelgm into her open thermos
on her desk next to Len Roberts'.
Maybe I could go hunting
with Jeffrey Skinner's Uncle Joe
or put on a cashmere suit
and go back to Akron, Ohio
with Philip Levine from Detroit.

But this poem needs to be written
about playing ring-a-leave-e-o
in gangways in the old neighborhood,
where rats are the only scare
lurking in dark corners
between buildings where we play on
past nine o'clock while lovers
embrace in dark passageways
outside doors that remain unlocked
throughout the night.

It's the first time in forty years
the White Sox will play in the series,
and for seven days, Chicago will forget

that America is at the helm of the world

with Dwight D. Eisenhower,
that rock 'n' roll is just four-years old,
and Chryslers and Cadillacs wear
wings for taillights.
It's a time when young girls roller skate
while we play fast pitching until dusk,
and little boys in Davy Crockett hats
play jacks on treeless streets
under six thousand, city stars
without ozone alerts and Laurie Dann.

It's a place where teen-age gals
slow dance in poodle skirts,
bobby socks and Angora sweaters
with older guys in Brylcreem-slicked hair
who finger snap to "Mack the Knife"

while they doo-wop around
push-button Dodges with fuzzy dice
and "Bobby loves Pidge"
air brushed on both sides.

For one week we won't care about
Gidget and Little Joe and two monkeys
hurling through space over New Jersey,
New York, Ohio and Illinois
and the rest of the forty-six states
where Dinah Shore launches
good-night kisses to us all
beneath the mid September, Russian moon.

ELIZABETH STREET

I went back to a place
where we used sewer covers for bases
and crushed waxed cups for baseballs,
a place peopled with names like Aiellinello,

Petrelli and Pascucciello.
But now there is an empty lot
where we once lived
filled with abandoned cars

with no license plates and broken bottles,
and three-bedroom lofts
where that nameless, factory wall
once hid like a secret

behind a cold-water walk-up.
For ten summers the fire hydrant
flushed high fliers made
with tires and two-by-fours.

I swam along street curbs
filled from backed-up sewers
until the police came
with their monkey wrenches.

Where have the Italian feasts gone,
the marching, oom-pah band on Sunday mornings
and Santa Maria Addolorata's procession

of religious icons that I was lifted up to kiss

for just one dollar?
And where is Addante's grocery store
where we pitched pennies until dusk
under a canopy to escape the widening June sun

already burning away thoughts of school,
and the old man yelling, "Bunch of potatoes"
on a horse-driven wagon filled with vegetables
in front of Rosa's candy store

where we bought black licorice sticks,
Kayo, and a candy bar all for fifteen cents?
All this made way for a gray, lifeless street
erased into an anonymity of lives gone past.

JUST NOT FAST ENOUGH

I tied a league ball in it, roped it
around twice with jute twine and greased it
with Vaseline before putting it between
my mattress and box spring each fall.
By April, my baseball glove
molded for another season.
When spring came, the days rang:
"Hey, batter, batter; swing batter, swing!"
I swung a Duke Snyder Adirondack,
but I was Louis Aparicio at the plate --
a singles hitter and fast,
a sure steal on the base paths.
In one game, the rain fouled up
my fifth stealing attempt,
and second base became a buoy.
My father and I navigated
out of the bog in his new '64 Oldsmobile,
until he asked about my muddy spikes... .
We torpedoed across traffic
and slid across shoals. He popped the trunk,
hurled my spikes high in the air.
I watched them descend,
the long, white laces twisting
in slow-motion, my mitt tied to them.
They hit the street with a dull splash,
and I held my breath an instant,
an eternity; as if dreaming, I dodged
the gloom of headlights bearing down
in an attempt to swipe. The whole season
disappeared beneath a semi-trailer
five times.

JIM'S MOM

I went up to Jim's door
the way I always did on summer mornings,
rang his door bell twice and waited.
But this time the window sheers parted
slightly, and Jim's mom opened the door
wearing only a silky half-slip and brassiere.
The shell of the wall phone
pressed against her ear
and long blond hair wet from bathing.

She said Jim wasn't home,
and I was embarrassed by her large
green eyes that flashed no hint of awkwardness,
by her body like one of those models
in a lady's lingerie section
of the mail order catalogue
I kept hidden in a chest of toys.

Perhaps it was my stuttering
or her understanding of a boy's gawking
that made her laugh,
but my body flushed down to my toes.
And I ran home burned by the moment.

WEB OF MEMORY

When Albert Witkins uncorked
the bottle, and they scattered
across our fifth grade classroom,
the girls danced the tarantella
upon their desks
while we ripped off spider legs for fun,
swallowed one whole
on a double dare.
That day we didn't know
that the moment they hatch from eggs
they can spin their death designs,
that their fine, silk thread
can hold 4,000 times their weight.
Now I know the quiet
of obsessive weavers,
how the weight of memory
is held in a soundless spin.

A LOSS OF SYMMETRY
(for Richard Zabransky)

Snow falls where cars sleep
in single file under lamplight
burning long into the night. Maples and elms
moan in a mad duet, and the light
hurtles somewhere else at light speed.

Once we watched each crystal explode
into an eternity upon the glass.
You said each fractal held a replica of itself --
a hexagon of reflections
in a kaleidoscope of mirrors.
Only the moon lingered, its pale light insisting
without confidence, borrowed from one last star.

Tonight I wake to the sound of steam
knocking like a metal lung
while moonlight dozes on my floor, and plows
rumble from their sleep to shoot white dust,
like an opiate, into the veins of Chicago.

IN THE CROSS HAIRS

For five days the buck hung
from the wrought-iron grate,
a large, brown buck heavy with muscle.
Its eyes held the look of an animal
about to be shot.

Benedetti, the pharmacist
with a half-dozen hunting dogs
smelling of musk-rank fur,
worked his knife in its belly,
unknitted tendons before my eyes.

It wasn't until the fifth day that someone
complained about the stench and sound
of the chainsaw grinding through bone,
the head that lay on the front stoop all evening,
deciduous antlers hacked from the skull.

I stood like a child
under a pale gray, Midwestern sky
deep in November.
The neighbor's cats kept their distance.
The air filled with pity and thanksgiving.

WHAT MEDALS MEAN
*(No one looks at you as you pass
because you're a deadman until you return.)*

You're on the next search-and-destroy patrol
somewhere near a river.
You feel only the heat and your weariness,
the humidity and your thirst.
You can't see through the squall,
but you keep walking through the gray sheets,
beneath a canopy of contorted vegetation,
along some twisted, dirt road. You're aware
of the sucking mud under your boots,
the elephant grass and the leeches.
And you're thinking ambush
and mines, about removing the tape
from the spoon of your grenade.
No one talks about the cobras and vipers,
the mosquitoes like an artillery burst,
the rioting stillness that follows.
You've seen a thousand nameless places,
and each time it's no different:
you fear getting lost,
that your weapon won't work.

But it's the quota that propels you on...
and you drag the bodies out in a row
to be photographed, then searched...
and you'd rather be on the perimeter
than riding an assault wave through this camp
because you're the one escaping this time,
smelling of smoke, gun powder and death,
heli-lifted for a Purple Heart.

A.W.O.L.

It's always the same dream:
the ambushers about to take aim,
the M-16 just out of reach,
the parachute slit open at the seams.

You come as close to death as you can,
and yet you stay alive in a free-fall nightmare
where you disappear into a vast sleep
in a mob of mangroves,

the pause button on your future depressed.
It's always that way. Before you blank out,
your life passes by, stands corrected
and remembered as a story truly yours

and no one else's. The medic reassures you
that you're not going to die, not yet.
He gives you another chance
where you are in control.

MAKING SURE THE DOORS ARE LOCKED

Sometimes, in the middle of the night,
I rise from sleep
and check the doors.
I go to my children's rooms,
listen to their breathing
escaping ahead of their dreams.

I know what it's like to safeguard their lives
with deaf eyes,
to think about the car idling on the corner
with its lights off,
the veil of ice on the pond,
the knife pressed against the palm.

This is the way it is waking night after night
in an arena of silence
while the refrigerator rehearses coldness,
and my wife sleeps with the voice of the wind,
leaving nothing to tell me where she's been,
where she's going.

BUBBIE

I can see her escaping Russia
like a small bird breaking formation
over unfamiliar terrain,
carrying her belongings in wooden wagons
across the Ukraine
under a roof of vagrant stars,
sleeping beneath shawls of leaves.
She bartered away possessions
salvaged from her hotel
ransacked by the Bolsheviks,
giving up an old world to find a new one
eight thousand miles away.

It was the prelude of a new decade,
and the world lay before her
like a matryoshka.
In America she gave up her Russian name,
and though she spoke no English,
she learned the language of a new place
while keeping the old alive.

I feel for her even now,
coming so far to everything and having nothing,
bringing with her the voice of an old country
that comes with quiet suffering.
The great war had murdered her family

with gas and guns, and for years
she remained silent as a sleepwalker
about their deaths.
Her husband died too before I was born.
She seldom mentioned his name,
and I did not know how to ask.

I still hear her voice,
sometimes unexpectedly from my son,
a voice searching in soft, broken tones
for the right word,
mispronouncing a vowel or consonant.
She would have called him "doll face."
He is the only one to carry our name.

AFTER HIS WITNESSING
AN ARGUMENT WITH MY FATHER

(for Geoffrey Glen)

I tell my son there are things
one should never say, hurtful words
like liar and cheat.

The heart holds whatever it hears
for a long time, I say.
The tongue is the mind's fist.

I want to find the right words
to make the difference
for the wrong ones,

if recovering from them is possible,
to tell him some things about my heart
I have never said to anyone.

I can tell what it felt like
to carry his grandmother
down the stairs after she died,

how once while sitting by her bedside
I was punched into silence
as I watched her sip

from an imaginary teacup,
how each day is an act of forgiveness,
that the mind will know

only what it has learned
and is last to discover
what the heart has known forever.

But I know this talk is for me.
The metaphor bleeds through the words
while he stares out the passenger's window.

BIRTH OF AN ANGEL
(for Suzanne Elizabeth)

The first big snow of the year
bursts with laughter in the backyard,

the forsythia and dogwood capsizing
under the weight where his daughter

plays in a white maze of discovery,
her small arms sweeping wings

under a moonswept sky.
He feels creation in his heart,

the mill wheel spin,
the birth of a child without sin.

A million hexagons dance from heaven,
a mysterious map of the universe

hidden in each eye
spiralling toward infinity,

while the weak December sky
promises miracles,

white-washes the land
where she is signalling an angel,

throwing curveballs every which way,
the pure, delicate arcs

bridging the two of them
in a milky circle of light.

MOON HORROR

Once I saw the moon
drift up as if balanced
by invisible legs.

I saw it melt, then freeze,
lose itself like a face
vanishing at night,
like white fire fallen to ash.

I feared this most:
this white wingless stone
drifting alone.

I stood quietly, afraid
of what infinitely
surrounded it -- those things
older than love and death.

About the Author

Glen Brown was born in Chicago and received his formative education there. He earned an M.A. at the University of Utah and a B.A. at Northeastern Illinois University. Recipient of numerous poetry awards, he is currently a creative writing and literature teacher at Lyons Township High School in La Grange and a composition instructor at the College of DuPage in Glen Ellyn, Illinois. He is a martial artist, musician, and father of two young children.

About the Artist

Chris Grodoski is a talented Art student at Illinois Weslyan University.